Class struggle and mental health
live to fight another day

Published by
FREEDOM PRESS
84b Whitechapel High Street, London
E1 7QX and
LIBCOM

www.freedom
press.org.uk

www.libcom.org

Printed 2015

ISBN 978-1-904491-24-8

This essay was first published online in 2014 following a series of discussions which occurred on the forums of libcom.org. It was printed in the US by Edmonton Small Press Association in 2014. First UK print edition.

Printed in Great Britain by Imprint Digital

A Note on terminology

The editors of this pamphlet tend not to use the words "activist" or "activism" to describe our class struggle activities. This is a for a variety of semantic and political reasons. However we have chosen to use these terms in the pamphlet because:

1. We know many dedicated class warriors do use such terms
2. For stylistic reasons it makes more sense than using the terms "militants," "comrades," "revolutionaries," etc., over and over again (a group of words in themselves which carry their own complicated connotations).

For a more in-depth discussion of such terminology (which, in itself, may have implications for the mental health of those actively committed to the class struggle), see "Give Up Activism" (available online at: libcom.org/library/give-up-activism).

Similarly, we've used the word libertarian in its historical sense: referring to the anti-state wing of the socialist movement. Obviously, it's a travesty that the right is trying to claim such terminology as their own. It goes without saying that we are opposed to the 'libertarianism' of the Libertarian Party, the Tea Party movement and other free-market ideologues.

First edition (2015)

This book was edited and brought together by two people who are active on the Libcom.org website (and who, along with most other contributing writers, prefer to remain anonymous). See other writer/illustrator credits on Page 38.

Introduction

This piece of writing comes out of a series of discussions which occurred on the forums of libcom.org.

It was repeatedly raised that depression, mental illness, and emotional stress are very common amongst libertarian political activists.

Furthermore, suffering from mental illness while politically active often comes with its own set of complications.

Sometimes the wider anarchist/ activist community is supportive and helpful. Other times, we can feel just as alienated amongst fellow anarchists as we do from the rest of capitalist society. With that in mind, the goal of this pamphlet is to offer some advice on what's generally helpful in maintaining overall mental health.

We don't, however, want to pretend for a second that this pamphlet is a substitute for professional medical advice.

While we're critical of certain aspects of mental health treatment, if you're suffering from severe depression or considering hurting yourself, please speak to someone immediately.

Living with depression isn't easy. Far too often, on a societal as well as interpersonal level, mental health issues are ignored — or worse, written off with sufferers being blamed as weak or just overreacting. Aside from the personal sense of alienation that often accompanies mental illness, the institutions of capitalist society offer sufferers very little control over their treatment.

Mental illness treatment is atomised and commodified, complete with hierarchy, coercion and the pressures of budgets, profit, and, bureaucracy.

Mental health facilities in schools are woefully lacking and while there's no problem calling off work because you're physically ill, very few employers have provisions for short or long-term mental health leave. Hospitals and mental health institutions often embody the very worst of institutional power.*

It's imperative, then, that the class struggle community take issues of mental health seriously. Mental health should be discussed and there ought to be networks where sufferers can turn when they need support.

We hope that this book can provide a start to that sort of thing taking shape.

We do wish to stress again, however, that this is not a substitute for the support and advice of trained medical professionals.

---

*This is not, we should add, an attack on workers in the medical industry. Many of them are extremely dedicated to the socially useful elements of the job – indeed, this is often what attracted them to the field in the first place. However, this still doesn't overcome the structural constraints of the industry or the fact that, as workers, they still operate within the framework of capitalist social relations.

General advice

When suffering from depression the first thing to remember is that you're by no means alone. Depression is something experienced by many, many individuals who are involved in class politics. Life in general is stressful. Being involved in politics is stressful (whether you're involved in an active group or an isolated militant). So it's not surprising that many of us suffer from depression.

If you're feeling depressed, the main advice we offer is to talk to someone. While we hope reading this helps, it's far more important to find someone to talk to. Ideally, talk to someone in person. In our collective experience, talking to someone else directly provides the best option.

But if you can't talk to someone in person, talk to someone on the phone. Online forums can provide help in a number of ways, but if you're thinking of hurting yourself and there's no one around you feel comfortable speaking to in person, call a helpline. A second, related point is that class politics are about solidarity and helping each other.

There's nothing wrong with reaching out when you need it. Whether we suffer from depression or not, we all need to discuss our feelings and emotions. It not only helps us as individuals, but strengthens us as a movement when we develop a healthy culture of discussion and support.

So if you need to talk to someone, that's okay. Part of the reason we get involved in politics is because we want to make the world a better place. That means most activists are more than happy to speak to a comrade who's in need of some emotional support, so don't be afraid to ask.

Sometimes being involved in class politics brings a sense of solidarity and purpose. For many people, feeling like they're helping their communities or making the world a better place brings great personal satisfaction. However, if politics are bringing more stress than enjoyment, take a step back. If you need a few months away from a political project or a group you're involved with, that's okay.

Similarly, don't over-extend yourself. It's not good anarchist practice when one person carries too many responsibilities in a group and it's certainly not good practice in terms of mental health.

Be realistic about how much time you can dedicate to a project and be open with others when you need help. If you're not getting the assistance you need, speak to the others involved, let them know, and allow them the opportunity to step up. Ultimately, however, don't feel the burden is on you to make things work.

Despite our revolutionary commitment, it's important to have other outside interests. It's beneficial to have parts of your life that aren't explicitly political and to relate to people who may not identify as politicos. Hobbies and sports, for example, are another way to find people who share common interests and who can be a trusted ear if you're feeling down.

They're also a good way to relieve stress and take what can often be a much-needed break from contemplating the ills of global capitalism. If you're feeling overwhelmed politically, it's worth looking into what sort of clubs, societies, classes, and meet-up groups are available in your area. Things like music and art, as well, often provide outlets to release your emotions and stay positive. As one of our contributors writes:

> Something I've found very useful is to add something creative into my life. Whether you're depressed or not, everyday life can be a bit soul destroying in terms of tangible achievements sometimes.
>
> I find it really helpful to have something that I've worked on, that I can say, 'Hey, I did that!' It doesn't have to be anything complex. Baking a cake even, something that you can take credit for yourself. It's a really good distraction from the background noise, something to focus on. I used to play guitar, losing myself in practicing a piece of music until I got it right.
>
> It doesn't really matter what it is, but that combination of being absorbed in a process and being able feel that you've accomplished something or learnt something new is really positive and affirming."

In a wider sense, it's important to be aware of your ups and downs. Depression is often cyclical and, much as possible, it's important to find ways to manage that cycle. Being aware of what in your life (and the world around you) triggers your depression is an important part of finding strategies to deal with it.

If you begin to feel depressed, undertake whatever strategies you've found to be helpful. Speak to a trusted friend. If possible, take a few days off work or school. Send apologies to meetings. If you find arguing with right-wingers on the internet keeps you up at night, turn off your computer. Get some extra sleep if that's what you need. But if you find staying in bed all day brings down your mood, make that extra effort to get outside and enjoy some fresh air. Take some time for yourself and focus on staying healthy and positive.

Finally, it's important understand depression as an illness. Society often ignores the fact that mental illness is an illness. (It's no problem calling off work with the flu and need a day to recover. But how many employers are accommodating if an employee calls off because they're feeling depressed and need a day to recover?).

One of the worst aspects of depression is that it leaves sufferers feeling guilty for being depressed, thus causing more depression. Suffering from depression is a very common illness and one which is exacerbated by the world in which we live.

We needn't feel guilty about it. And, again, it's important to talk to others to find ways to manage how depression affects us not only in our darker moments, but in our wider lives.

Management strategies

Community involvement
Many people find that helping others helps them to deal with their depression. An example that often comes up is feeding homeless people. While this is good advice, try to get involved in an already existing project and don't take on more than is emotionally sustainable for you.

Also, try not to make it explicitly political. The idea here is to help others, not turn it into a political project. While giving out food for the evangelical church down the road is probably not the best idea, there are lots of liberal community groups one can get involved with. There are plenty of other options, too: after-school programs, libraries, support work and advocacy, litter removal, volunteering at a hospice or hospital, work with ex-convicts, etc. As always, if you feel community work is causing more stress than it's alleviating, scale back your involvement.

Exercise
Anecdotal as well as clinical research often claims that exercise is just as, if not more, effective than anti-depressants. The problem, however, is taking that initial step to get started. Sometimes it's helpful to find a friend and sign-up to a course together. Alternatively, make yourself a schedule, selecting a specific time to go for a walk, ride a bike, lift weights, or play basketball.

While we think it's always important to have activities outside of politics, there are many possibilities to integrate exercise into your political life. Many organisations offer self-defense courses, for example. If that's not your forté, you can start a regular exercise session within your political group or trade union. And it doesn't have to be super formal either—a weekly pick-up game of basketball or football/soccer in the park is fine, too. Finally, you could consider doing a charity run. It'll probably be liberal, but there are plenty of at least partially worthy causes out there which might help to motivate you to get out there and train.

Finally, remember that there's no need to undertake especially strenuous exercise. As one of our contributors puts it, "Walking works wonders, it's exercise, but it also re-engages you with a real physical world... plus it's still possible to discuss while walking!"

Drugs/alcohol:
While there's nothing inherently wrong with drugs and alcohol in a broad sense, understanding how they affect you and your mental health is a really important part of managing your emotional state. If alcohol tends to make you depressed or upset (either while drinking or afterward), avoid it.

Similarly, psycho-active drugs like ecstasy or acid can have a negative effect on your mental state. And downers (certainly opiates) are probably not a good idea.

But, of course, this can go either way. Everyone reacts differently to drugs. Everyone finds their different ways of coping. The key is to be aware and conscious of the effect drugs have on your body and your mental state. Many people report that, when used proportionately, alcohol or marijuana can help them relax at the end of the day. However, if you're finding you can't get through the day without it or if your recreational drug use is exacerbating your depression, it's probably best avoided.

Finally, we again wish to emphasise that this pamphlet is not a substitute for professional help. While mental health workers have contributed in the writing process, we don't claim to have the expertise to speak definitively on the above issues. As always, if your depression is severe or you're thinking of hurting yourself, speak to someone ASAP.

Stephanie McMillan

Personal accounts

66 The key thing for me was to allow people to help...

I used to over-analyse to the point of minutiae why I get depressed. I have had
periods of depression for as long as I can remember and sometimes they've been
utterly disabling. I've come to the conclusion that there is no actual answer; I think I
was looking for a definitive cause so I could definitively put a stop to it.

I suspect there's a whole combination of factors, probably brain chemistry comes
into it, emotional trauma — I had an abusive childhood, which I know had an
enormous influence on my thought processes growing up, which then carried over
into adulthood.

I'm never sure whether having radical politics is a help or a hindrance; sometimes
when I'm having a bad time, the general sorry state of the world just adds to it. I call
them my "It's all too big" days, when I can't deal with what's going on in the world.

On the other hand, at other times I find it a positive resource, knowing that I'm not
the only person who thinks we should be doing it differently, it's kind of optimistic.
I'm sure that societal pressures come into play too, life is incredibly stressful, it's
hardly surprising that it would have a detrimental effect on my mental health.

I also think that depression is sometimes a perfectly normal reaction to traumatic
events; I don't feel that it's reasonable that people should carry on as normal when
dreadful things happen to them. Anyway, I stopped trying to find a magic bullet and
started looking at it as a mostly manageable condition.

One aspect that I'd like to touch on is the incredibly isolating nature of depression.
Largely I've managed to overcome this, but it took a long time. When I was younger
I just felt so lonely in my own head. I found it absolutely impossible to discuss this
with anyone.

It's got a little better, I feel. People are more receptive to talking about mental
health these days, but back then it felt like there was such a huge stigma associated
with it that I didn't dare disclose how I was feeling.

The way I grew up I developed enormous trust issues and I didn't want to expose
myself to letting anyone very close to me emotionally. I find it quite difficult now
to fully understand what was going on in my head back then, but I think that in an
effort to shield myself from getting hurt I disallowed myself the opportunity to let
anyone help me. It's not as if I didn't have lots of friends, but as soon as they got too
close I would run a mile.

Looking back I can see that there were lots of people who offered their hands to
help me, but I wouldn't take the chance to let them.

I also had a crippling insecurity that if I let people fully understand what made me
tick that they wouldn't like it, and would judge me or reject me. I have no idea what

it was that I thought I should have been but I had a debilitating sense that people would find me wanting.

The only way I got out of this was to actually let someone in. I actually sought medical help at one point, but because I tried doing it on my own without any support, or even letting anyone know I was doing it, it failed dismally.

In my case it took a friend who was just too tenacious to let me get away with running for the hills when I thought that would be my best option, someone who recognised my depression, who'd been there, and with great sensitivity chipped away at the wall I had constructed, a wall which I thought I was protecting myself with.

Then I found that once I'd let someone help me it was far easier to let others do so. So the key thing for me was to allow people to help me. It meant admitting that I was vulnerable, which was so frightening, but it turned out that there were people who cared about me and wanted to help.

I look back at that young woman that I was with some sadness now. I put up a good front for public view, but I was so incredibly lonely and my loneliness and insecurity just fed off each other. And I find it so unfathomable that I would do this to myself because it's really not the way I am now.

So, everyone's different and my experiences don't necessarily relate to anyone else's but I think it's really vital that people don't try to deal with their depression on their own. Sometimes it's really hard to ask for help, and although not everybody is able to offer it, it is really worth persevering.

A few thoughts on seeking professional help: I found in my experience and through talking to others that the mental healthcare profession can be really hit or miss. It can depend on having a sympathetic doctor (I had one GP basically telling me to stop whining and get a job once) and what is available in your area.

Also, it's not a one size fits all thing, some treatments or programs work better for some than others. I had group therapy at 19 which was awful.

There was no way I was going to sit in a room full of strangers, most of whom seemed to be in a worse state than me and disclose deeply personal information. I used to have anxiety attacks just thinking about it.

In my experience, if one approach isn't working, try something else. I know this is problematic because what is available is so dependent upon what healthcare services are available in your area and the last thing you need when you are depressed is to shop around and have to fight to get the care you need (which is where having support is useful).

It can be really dispiriting to seek help and find it's not working. See if you can find an advocacy group in your area who'd be willing to help you cut through the bureaucracy and honestly show you what treatments are available.

66 To refuse the feeling that I only deserved bleakness...

Depression is not always feeling sad. Most of the time it is feeling nothing. If I shut down my emotions then it becomes a weight that presses down on my entire life but one that I can almost pretend isn't there as I listlessly stare at a screen, without the patience to get to the end of the webpage I am 'reading'.

I flick between websites and inane games while a video plays. When you don't pay attention to anything you don't mind watching the same video five or six times in a few days. I don't call my friends; I know I have nothing to say to anyone. I don't want them to know how shit my life is. I can barely sleep. The only way I can get myself to work is the sheer terror of losing my job and being evicted.

So after a week of sleepless nights, of screaming at the shower as it runs hot and cold in the morning I finally hit the weekend. I drink, but I can barely manage a beer before falling asleep on Friday nights. I don't sleep through the weekend and catch up, if it were possible, on my sleep. I laze around my flat. I look at the boxes that I haven't unpacked yet, I've been here for months. I didn't manage to unpack them at my last flat either.

The flat is a mess, nothing is organised and everything is covered in dust. I hate living in shit but I can't seem to find the energy to do anything about it. Every few days I do the washing up and if there's a stain in the toilet I chuck some bleach down it. Apart from that I don't clean or maintain my flat. I don't do much for myself. I have a shower each day before work.

I've grown a beard because I can't face shaving and my hair has grown out because I can't face looking for a barber and trying to talk about what I want. My friends sometimes mention that I seem a little down, but mostly we all just ignore it. I don't see them much anyway so I can usually summon up something approaching who I used to be.

I've always had a dark sense of humour so I feel like the stream of gallows humour isn't going to upset people too much. I see no future. Every day is just putting off the crushing endless weight. Everything I do is not good enough.

Terror gets me to work and nervous energy keeps me going through the day, just about. I don't make plans, I don't want to see anyone, nothing really cheers me up and I don't want to bring down the people that care about me.

When someone mentions visiting me or invites me somewhere I feel unable to cope with it, I can't see myself having the energy to buy a train ticket, get to the station, or tidy my flat. It's beyond me to phone a friend most of the time, actually seeing one seems almost impossible.

As long as you tell people that you are fine it's ok. Even when I have openly told my boss everything is falling apart she offers me bland assurances rather than going through the effort of helping me; then she can hear the sound of her own voice as she tells me irrelevant anecdotes. I have mostly given up trying to get help and I can't even manage to get angry about it.

Depression makes you feel alone, it makes you feel as if you will never get better, it makes you think that this is how it is for you, it turns you against yourself, it shuts down your ability to fight it. My whole life is stripped down. This dullness that lays upon everything. I feel crushed and drained. I feel like I have to keep going, but I have no idea where, I can't see how anything will change or improve.

I had been a heavy drinker a few years previous but I am so exhausted that I have pretty much stopped drinking because I am tired of pouring it away. One glass of wine was thrown away after three nights of attempting to drink it. There are bottles of decent wine in my cupboard waiting for me to feel capable of drinking a glass.

There are books on the shelf that I don't feel I will ever read, considering that a page's worth of text is more than I have managed for weeks or months. I have films I haven't watched, I know that I won't be able to concentrate long enough to enjoy them. Three Sundays in a row I was almost in tears, saying out loud "Life isn't supposed to be like this."

I was at the end of my tether, with a nudge from a friend I called in sick, I went to the doctor for anti-depressants the same day. I spent almost all of that first week asleep, I was exhausted in every sense, but there was a sense of satisfaction.

After more than a year of barely feeling alive I had finally managed to refuse the feeling that I only deserved bleakness, I could laugh at how ridiculous this realisation was; but I was able to start seeing it as one of the most important moments in my life. It's been a while now, but things are looking a lot better.

I don't have most of what I want, and the depression still comes, but I know what it is, I know that it isn't me. I had been under the shadow of depression for a very long time, so long that I had no real idea who I was without it, if there was anything else. Over the course of years it had taken more and more from me until that last year; which apart from a few moments of joy, was lifeless; joyless and it was me, alone with my depression, having trouble realising that there was anything in the world.

❝ Be Good to Yourself

I was diagnosed with dysthymia when I was 13, the same year I learned who Emma Goldman was. I tried committing suicide with the cables that came with my PlayStation. My mother found me in my closet with a terrible excuse for a noose wrapped around my neck.

Ninth grade: vice principal overreacted to me being in the library during my free period. I was a hair away from leaping into the stairwell in my high school. Instead, I went to the social worker, who called my mother, four hours later, diagnosed with regular ol' depression.

Freshman year of college, first month: I felt rejected by my peers, crammed as many Prozac as I could fit into my mouth, watched five minutes of Glee, walked onto the quad near the women's center, hid behind a bush and called someone.

I honestly can't remember who. Came to at a crappy hospital in the city, was given charcoal to drink so I could puke the pills back up, thought "This is pretty fucking goth of me to puke up pure black." Then was admitted to the shitty hospital's even shittier psych ward for two and a half of the most agonizing days of my life. Had I not wanted to kill myself before, I certainly wanted to inside that psych ward.

"They should have taken you to the children's hospital," the on-campus psychologist said to me, "You would have felt more at ease." More rejection by my peers when I came back to campus a week later. Can't stand Glee. Diagnosed with severe depression.

Sophomore year of college, the entire academic year up to around March: I was raped the summer between freshman and sophomore year. From August on, took any drug I could find, drank anything that was given to me, my breakdown was more intense than any hardcore song.

Finally fucked it up spectacularly with my then-live in partner, took as many Tylenol as I could, turned on the TV and laid down on my couch. Woke up hours later in the worst pain of my life, realised my mom was coming up to visit, didn't tell her nor anyone else about this suicide attempt until about a week later, when I went to the on campus psychologist again.

Finally started going to an amazing therapist on the wealthy side of the city, diagnosed with major depressive disorder and post traumatic stress disorder. Currently a senior in college, I haven't acted on a suicidal urge since February 2011.

That isn't to say I don't have urges, I do, but I've trained myself to not act on them whatsoever. My depression will always be with me, until the day I die. I've accepted this. I feel no shame in it. It runs in the family, both sides. It was pretty much doomed from my disjointed, yet happy, childhood. How the fuck did I make it to 22?

Realise that your mental illness/disorder/whatever it may be is not the same as others'. Nor should it be. There is no strict adherence to what your personal mental illness is going to be like. It's more of a "loose guideline" sort of deal.

Much like food poisoning, you know when you have it. Unlike food poisoning, shitting or puking your brain out doesn't get rid of it, I think. There is no one way to treat your mental illness. Some people take any assortment of meds, some meditate, some take vitamins, some smoke weed, some do nothing or everything.

Don't fucking shame anyone about how they manage their mental illness because that's just fucking rude as hell. I know that my money (rather, mommy dearest's kickass insurance) lines the pockets of fucked-up rich fucks, but that money is well fucking spent for me to survive in this twisted pisshole known as planet earth.

I'm a privileged little fuck for having what I have to treat my mental illness. I know I have thousands of weird chemicals keeping me functional, but frankly, it fucking works. Diversity of tactics.

Keep your mind open to other ideas regarding treatment and management, but always exercise caution. If your gut instinct says, "hey this sounds safe" go for it. Do your research regardless, though.

When it comes to illegal drugs, keep a diligent eye. I know that I can tolerate weed and booze, and I should avoid pretty much everything else. It sucks I can't trip the light fantastic, but thems the breaks. If you're concerned about your usage of any drug, talk to your psych, doctor, friend, anyone you feel safe with.

When it comes to your mental illness, tell those you feel comfortable telling. If anyone gives you shit about it, try and stay away from that person. And if anyone uses it against you, call that asshole out. That shit ain't right.

My usual rule is: replace 'depression' with 'lupus.' If what that person is saying is now fucked up, it was fucked up to begin with. Self. Care. Eat a bag of tortilla chips. Masturbate. Get a tattoo. Whatever makes you happy, keep a mental scrapbook of it (or an actual one!), do it when shit gets tough. Treat yo'self.

Realise that things you might find really ridiculous or goofy might make you feel better. I think meditation is cheesy as all get out, but it works pretty well for me. Sometimes I post my hard lows on a message board I frequent (they have a designated section for that, actually).

It's embarrassing and I hate it, but the advice I've gotten has really helped me out of some terrible places. Solidarity. You aren't the only one going through this. Even statistically, at this moment, someone is feeling something pretty damn close to how you feel. Sorry Morrissey, but Somebody Can Possibly Know How You Feel.

Among your organisations, if you feel that you need to share that you're going through some tough shit, share it. But keep it on a need-to-know basis and possibly out of public view. It's usually the best. If you don't feel safe, don't do it. You can't go to every march. You can't burn down every cop car. You can't attend every meeting. This is perfectly okay. Sometimes you need to stay in bed.

You may not be the most perfect radical, but you don't have to be. But socializing can be good. I sometimes have to push myself to go to one fucking rally. Even if it's me hiding in a crowd, being surrounded by people can sometimes help.

Sometimes fellow radicals say really terrible shit regarding mental illness. If they're near and dear, tell them directly (or through a safe third party). Maybe surreptitiously post something on Facebook about mental illness stigma. Or scream at that fucker if they just don't get it (use this as a last resort).

Mental illness sometimes just happens. There may be no rhyme or reason to it. This isn't your fault. Could be genetics, could be fate, could be something in the water. Stay safe, smash the state, be good to yourself.

66 My sensitive heart...

I've struggled with depression, anxiety, the consequences of substance misuse and chemical dependence, and eventually was diagnosed with bipolar NOS ("not other specified", i.e. that my bipolar symptoms do not fit neatly into the categories bipolar I or II).

I am not just my diagnosis though. I'm a fierce queer woman of color and an anarchist. I'm a fighter and I'm a survivor. I have anarchy in my heart and in my writings. I am a relapsed political activist who has been involved in protests and demonstrations for a better world.

However I, like the rat in the cage pressing a lever to get sweet liquid or drugs, know what it's like to be an addict and to struggle with depression.

I grew up the oldest daughter from immigrant Chinese parents. Alienated with the suburban life, overwhelming political apathy, and conservatism as well as my own social anxiety and depression, I turned to substances, politics and music. I remember days I would frantically scour the cabinets at home for anything to bring a sweet release, any pill — yellow muscle relaxers, white sleeping pills, bottles of dissociatives and deliriants, anything to get high, to get away from this alienating suburban life.

Of course this all started as a happy accident. At 16, I unhappily tried to end my own life with some pills. Instead of needing to go to the hospital or having my parents realise what had happened, I had parental loving concern at the rash of hives I got and got mindblowingly, uncomfortably high.

After that, I experimented with numerous substances for seven years before being hospitalised for a manic/psychotic episode.

So what does a class-privileged misfit have to say about the working class and depression? I'm not even currently a part of any formal or class struggle organisations, instead picking and choosing protests to show up masked up in with my comrades by my side.

My sensitive heart wants to help others drained by depression and anxiety. Whether your heart beats fast in social situations or whether you can't sleep at night and stare at the numbers of time ticking by, I've been there.

I haven't been with you as you break down from anxiety in a bathroom stall, scared that other people will find you. I haven't been there with you holding your hair as you vomit from a night of trying to fit in. I haven't been there as you struggle out of bed and wish for suicide in the morning. But I wish I was there for you, comrade.

I wish I was there to tell you to take time for yourself. Slow down a little bit and practice mindfulness, meditation, yoga. Make yourself a cup of tea. It's okay if you hear voices or are so scared of some situations that you think you can't face them. What's not okay is letting it prevent you from being the beautiful bursting-to-live radical you are.

The world deserves to have you around because you are a great person. You deserve to sleep 6, 7, 8, or how many or little hours a night you need to function. You deserve to eat good food with good friends and family, chosen and biological. You deserve so much more out of life than this shitty broken ugly capitalist patriarchal system.

〟 I can't afford to wait until after capitalism has been abolished to be happy, and I doubt you can either.

Class struggle and depression: these two concepts are like mental buzzwords to me as they have both played a major role in defining who I am, as much as I hate to admit it.

I have never actually used the two of them in the same sentence because I never made a substantive connection between the two — class struggle is political, depression is personal. But when I saw the call for submissions to this text, I knew that there was probably a deep-rooted connection that is imperative to understand if we are going to effectively fight in the class struggle.

Unfortunately, but not coincidentally, many of us involved in the movement have suffered from depression and/or any number of emotional/psychological issues. Even worse, these are typically the factors which contribute to a range of internal problems in our organising work, and many times can lead to burnout.

So, how do we begin making the connection between depression and the class struggle, and to what end? I could begin by telling you my personal story, about my life-long battles with depression and the smorgasbord of related issues, but, as therapeutic as it may be, that would individualise what is in fact a societal problem.

Or I could begin by stating the obvious, that our emotional and psychological problems are consequences of social stratification, patriarchy, and the other dysfunctional elements of society, and follow this with a Marx quote. But many of us are already aware of the societal reasons why we are unhappy.

Just understanding this doesn't help much in finding a way of coping with the battles we face every single day, at least not for me. I personally can't afford to wait until after capitalism has been abolished to be happy, and I doubt you can either. Instead, I want to form a better understanding not just of how to understand what our problems are and what has caused them, but how we can use our anger to fuel our struggle. Or, to paraphrase the anarcho-punk band Crass, turn the nature of their oppression into the aesthetic of our anger.

In my experience, I've found that many of us understand the problem and do our best to make things better for ourselves — to make life comfortable at least — yet sometimes it's never enough. We try mainstream medicine and alternative medicine and low-cost therapy and the best therapy our city has to offer, sometimes we even read zines or commercial self-help books, but none of these seem to provide satisfying, long-term solutions.

I've learned that while there is no "cure" for the emotional and psychological issues which I have to cope with on a day-to-day basis, I can use my understanding of its root causes to engage in activity that makes the personal political, and that drives me into action, especially on bad days.

Having this understanding doesn't make me feel better, it just makes me angrier, but as a class struggle anarcho-syndicalist I have certainly learned what to do with my anger.

Perhaps this sounds cliché, but engaging in the class struggle is what keeps me driven, it helps me spring out of the feeling of drudgery when I'm at work, it gives me a solid network of couches to sleep on when I'm traveling, and it gives me the feeling of being connected with like-minded people in an otherwise alienating society.

Our organising work is not just a fight against the bosses, but it involves building a community of people who we are fighting alongside. When we support each other as we fight together, we're one step closer to curing depression.

66 Remember that there will be a day when the lights start to get turned back on again...

The problem I've found with depression is that... well, it's lifelong, and as such sneaks in and takes much of your life away. I'm not involved with any groups, I don't attend any meetings... I'm politically aware, yet have no real engagement with any campaigns.

Gradually, over the course of my life, I've withdrawn from more and more things. Depression isolates you. It isn't just being sad; it's a complete lack of hope or inclination, usually accompanied by misplaced and indefinable anxiety.

How do you take part in a struggle when you can't even see the point in changing your clothes? How do you attend a meeting or a protest, when just the idea of walking into a room full of people — or even leaving your house in the first place — fills you with cold-sweat fear?

Even if these are people you've known your whole life, it can drive an invisible wedge of humiliation and fear between you. I've driven people away from me, people I've loved, because I couldn't cope with who and what I become when I'm depressed.

When the depression is clinical, as mine is, you're told again and again that you are incapable of work, that your horizons must be lowered to take into account your actual abilities (versus your desired abilities).

So how can you take part in a struggle for workers when deep down inside you, you feel that you are not a worker, that you are a failure? How can you define yourself in the class struggle when you have been declared 'classless' in the worst way — you don't belong anywhere, except on medication...

How can you stand up in front of a group of friends and declare your heart is in the cause, when just last week you were shouting at everyone that the whole thing was bullshit and pointless — it's just all-round humiliating, makes you feel shallow and inconsistent. But it's not you, it's chemicals in your brain temporarily disrupting your patterns.

Groups like libcom.org are excellent for the likes of me. I didn't grow up around anyone politically aware or active. My parents were Tories. Luckily my grandparents were socialists, and though they died when I was young, they pointed me in the direction they could see I should be headed in. But depression has isolated me, and as a result I don't even know where to start...

My advice if you have depression? Flag it up. Speak out, not for pity, which you won't want anyway, but just as a fact that should be out there. Reclaim your depression as a part of your wiring — it's one of the reasons you are able to see the truths in the world.

Depression is part of us, otherwise evolution would've driven it out by now! It gives us new perspectives when we come out the other side, but the danger is that on the way through you retreat and push everyone away, so when you re-emerge there's no one to tell your insights to, which makes you isolated, withdrawn — and more prone to depression.

More importantly for those in groups who want to support depressives... keep an eye on them. Watch out for signs that depression is winning and that a feeling of pointlessness is taking over — not attending meetings, coming up with excuses not to socialise (most of my friends wouldn't know I was depressive — they'd just think I had a full timetable of other engagements, all of which are invented), withdrawing...

How to help? Remember that there will be a day when the lights start to get turned back on again, keep that person involved in any small way, so that when the lights go back on it's not embarrassing for them to re-emerge (I've found that to be the biggest problem — getting back involved makes you feel awful for dropping out).

Bring them stuff to read, fire them up. Music always helps, the lighthearted and the simple always helps. A cup of tea and some new music, together with a bit of tub-thumping rhetoric can re-ignite a tiny spark somewhere. Remember that we can still spot 'patronising'; treat us as the person you know we are, remember that our temporary insecurities will make us feel needy and pathetic. Make us feel useful (personally, when I'm depressed, long, drawn-out repetitive tasks work wonders for taking me away from myself!).

❝ The Personal is Political

Since becoming convinced of the need to overthrow capitalism and the state and replace it with a more just, egalitarian and sustainable system, I have made that struggle the primary focus of my life for over a decade.

When comrades cautioned me to slow down and take it easy in order to avoid burning out, I dismissed their advice. When others said they were burnt out, or needed time to recuperate and gather themselves, and took a step back from being directly involved in the movement, I inwardly thought that they lacked commitment, or had lost their conviction. Burnout, I thought, was a bourgeois luxury.

The last few years prior to writing this article have been probably the most difficult of my life — from the depression caused by failed romance, the death of some family members and the life-threatening illness of others, to physical and/ or mental health problems — certainly the last three or so months before I left for abroad had seen me hit an all-time low.

Ordinarily, under such circumstances I would have invested more of my time, energy and focus in political work in order to distract myself. But with my own political organisation going through somewhat of a crisis, this didn't seem to help; throwing up even more difficult questions with which I felt I had to deal.

Not knowing how to, and sometimes not feeling as though I had somewhere or someone to turn to for help and advice, or even for comfort, I frequently found myself turning to alcohol as a means of escape, dulling-down of the senses or just to pass the time.

Other times I simply found myself trying to sleep the day away, as though what I was experiencing was a bad dream from which, I hoped, I would soon awake. Feeling unable and unwilling to deal with external pressures I occasionally severed communication with other people and comrades, or at least couldn't bother myself to respond to attempts — however urgent — to reach me.

I mention this only because I have witnessed similar behaviour in other comrades and have concluded that such behavioural patterns are peculiar neither to myself nor to people with mental health diagnoses, but can be experienced and expressed, to varying degrees, by anyone.

Consequently, for the final few weeks or months before leaving South Africa I found myself unable to perform my duties or meet expectations. I faltered on mandates and constantly felt that I was letting myself, my comrades and, by extrapolation, the class and its struggle down.

This fed into a cycle of self-loathing, depression and inability to properly function on a personal or political level. Had I just been faced with a personal crisis, or just been faced with a political crisis I may well have been able to cope. After all, I'd been confronted by and overcome both before. But, finding myself at the intersection of the two, I was lost for a way out. As the old feminist dictum goes, "the personal is the political".

I was lucky to have been able to go to Brazil when I did, although that in itself brought new challenges, uncertainties and insecurities — both personal and political. But had I not, I'm not sure how I would have coped.

I think I narrowly avoided burning out which, I've seen, it can take years to recover from. Being abroad I had the opportunity of conversing with some truly knowledgeable and inspirational anarchist socialist militants that recounted similar experiences — of losing brilliant minds and militants to burnout, depression and addiction — reminding me that I was not alone and that, like everyone else, we socialists are human. We go through ups and downs, have good times and bad ones. Sometimes we cope, sometimes we don't.

This is maybe even more true of socialist militants, as not only are we living under the odious yoke of class society — with all that that entails — but we are actively trying to change it, against frightening odds. Perhaps even more so than socialists in general, could this be true of anarchist socialists, whose ideas and vision are even more alienated and isolated — contemporarily speaking — not just from the popular classes we seek to convince thereof, but from much of the rest of the left as well. In the case of anarchists in South Africa one could add to this political isolation from much of the left, our geographic isolation from most of the rest of the international anarchist movement — mostly concentrated in Europe and the Americas.

This political and geographic isolation can be compounded still when militants feel a real or perceived personal isolation as well, one sometimes even self-imposed. As with the popular classes as a whole, which fluctuate between periods of heightened class consciousness and combative class struggle, and periods of decline in both; so too might individuals go through periods of fluctuating levels of militancy or activity.

When class consciousness and struggle are at a low ebb, the popular classes become more susceptible to opportunist threats in their desperation to alleviate their own suffering and misery — from power-hungry politicians to parasitic organised religions and reactionary ideologies. So too may individual militants become more susceptible to the dangers posed by loneliness and depression, addiction and disillusionment that could be spurred on by the increased alienation and isolation of both themselves and their ideas in the context of decreased levels of consciousness, politicisation, and struggle.

It is in such a context of decreased class consciousness that we find ourselves today, and it is the accompanying threats faced by individual militants against which we need to guard. It's imperative that as individuals and organisations we understand these issues and that we actively seek to alleviate them as much as possible.

I don't claim to have easy answers, but simply having these discussions is surely a step in a positive direction. From there we can begin to build structures of support and develop our own capabilities, as individuals and as a movement, to create strategies for defeating burnout and keeping alive the flame of anarchist-socialist resistance.

❝ The revolution will wait for you.

The last time I went into the hospital was because of a mental crash that occurred while I was working at a school in the poor French town where I live with my wife and our son.

At the time I was very dedicated to my job and to my union. That year I'd been on strike many times, fighting against a director who was willing to fire the whole supervisory staff, of which I was an employee. I defended my colleagues on a daily basis and was under pressure every minute that I spent at work.

Unfortunately, I also had to fight against the kids. It was (and still is) a school with a very violent and confrontational environment. As an anarchist, it's not easy to yell at kids. But when a fight occurs, you don't make suggestions. You say something like, "I order you to drop the knife now!"

That's an extreme example, but it does mean you end up acting like a fucking cop, sometimes resorting to physical coercion. I can assure you that it makes you feel bad. This stress followed me home and I was always in bad mood. When I wasn't angry, I was depressed to the point I wanted to vanish off the planet.

I went to the doctor often and took time off work. Going out for a walk wasn't really a good idea as the inevitable yelling and street fighting only increased my stress. It came to the point that I had to take a month off, staying in my room, feeling totally crazy.

My doctor then sent me to a public mental health center. I accepted a stay of two weeks. It was difficult. What made me feel better was to help the other patients. I fed a woman who had refused to eat for three days, shared my cigarettes, tried to calm down a guy who was in crisis, and listened to the sad stories of other patients. The medical staff were cool with that. I wasn't trying to interfere, just trying to be kind in a very sad and unpleasant place.

Some comrades tried to reach me regarding union-related questions. I told trusted comrades about the situation, made it clear that my top priority was a healthy mental state, and gave up all responsibilities. I tried not to feel guilty about it.

Mental health has been a lifelong issue for me. I was first sent to a psychologist at age nine and again as a teenager. Even with this, I dropped out of school. It changed a bit a year later with my first job and my increasing interest in politics.

But the depression has always been there: the feelings of loneliness, the impression that my life has no meaning, that I will never feel serenity, and the often and all-too-real sentiment that I've lost touch with reality. This scared me to death sometimes.

Paradoxically, the only moments I've felt really good were when I took drugs. I started smoking pot at 12. I've done all the drugs I could try since. Can I say, today, that my mental issues are linked to my drug consumption and vice versa? Yes, of course. But it's taken me a long time to admit it.

When I got out of the mental health center, it didn't go well. I went back to work, took too many days off and finally got fired. I then decided to drop the union. The job was tough but I loved it and it was hard to accept that I wouldn't be a militant in the workplace. So I took a year to take care of my mental health and to find a profession that would fit my personality. I still have a psychologist and a psychiatrist who've helped me with every step. After one year of treatment, I've found another job. It's not the kind of work most people would enjoy, but I'm perfectly happy with it.

My family was the main reason I fought so hard to improve my situation. It was very painful for me to be unable to take care of them and support them through their own problems. I have to admit that we didn't tell our child about my issues while I was in treatment. I didn't want to scare him or make him sad. I will wait to tell him until the day that he will be able to understand.

I'm trying to be a strong person for my son, someone that he can count on. It's very hard sometimes. If I'm writing down my story, it's because I want to tell people with mental health issues that you have to accept your own weakness and seek the help you need. Keep faith in yourself and your loved ones.

You shouldn't feel guilty if you stop organising. Some people think they can forget their problems by giving all their time to activism. That's unrealistic. You can't expect mental stability from activism. If you are in a good organisation with good people they should understand that sometimes a comrade needs to quit union or political activities. If they don't, they don't deserve you.

I still have ups and downs. But I have identified those phases and I know that when I'm feeling bad it won't last very long. Now I have a lot more good moments than bad ones. I'm a mentally ill person; I have to live with that fact and it's fine. The pain is not as strong as it used to be and now I know where it comes from. Now I can make long-term plans for my life and I have even started to write a book!

While I was in the mental health center I created a kind of code of conduct and it helped a lot. Here it is: Psychologist and psychiatrist: Give the pain a name. You should have one person to talk to and one doctor to give you the right treatment. You have to be the one to choose them. Give them a try for a month. If you don't feel comfortable talking to them, try someone different.

You should try to think about your conversations with your psychologist once in a while (not too often) and be prepared with ideas that came to mind between meetings. In the case where you don't have anything to say, it's not bad at all. It's a part of the process. Don't feel ashamed or frustrated, those silences mean a lot.

It will take time to find good medical treatment. You will have to be patient before you feel better. If a treatment makes you feel bad, change it. We all react in different ways to medication. The most important thing is to feel stable. The pills you take won't make you a happy person. Stability is key. You need mental stability to think and to act rationally. Mental stability will help you identify the source of your pain. Your doctor should tell you what it is and you will talk about it. You will have a name for it. It will help you a lot for the next steps.

Avoid the guilt: Do one thing, be proud of it. If you're feeling so bad that you don't have the energy to do anything, accept it. You have to admit that you can't act as a stable person would. It's ok. But if you don't clean your living space, don't wash yourself and do nothing at all, you will start to feel even worse.

You should at least do one thing a day. Not necessarily something useful. Find one good guitar riff, write a few words in a personal diary, take a shower, vacuum your bedroom, watch a good movie, draw your pain... Take five to ten minutes to do one thing and give yourself some rest. Remember: you did something today and you will do one thing tomorrow... be proud.

If you have important things to do, write them down. Try to achieve one of these tasks per week. Just one per week. If you can't do it, that's ok. It only means that you're not ready yet. Maybe next week, maybe next month. Take the time you need. The whole idea is to avoid feeling guilty and to be proud of yourself. If you try and still can't do anything, you're still trying, you are a fighter. Be proud.

Activism: Only if you're feeling well. Maybe depression is linked to the capitalist system, to patriarchy, to the bad environment. Maybe not. We don't know when we will put an end to these systems of domination and destruction. Our depression won't wait.

You can spend your whole life in demonstrations, public meetings, going on strike or handing out flyers. It won't heal you. Most of the time you will be frustrated because whatever you do, it won't generally go the way you want. It won't go as far as you hope. Sometimes you will even fight against your own comrades. Sometimes something good will happen. In any case, it will take time and energy.

Depressive or not, it can be too much to give at certain points in your life. Sure, it can help to have friends who understand your politics. They can give you the strength to do incredible things, a true friendship and a community that shares your sense of solidarity. That's why you shouldn't hesitate: If you're feeling the need to take a break, take that break.

Anti-authoritarian politics is about freedom and you should feel free about your involvement. There's a huge difference between being unable to do stuff because you're not serious about it and being unable to do stuff because you can't.

A revolutionary activist should know that we need to be stable and rational to make good decisions. But the most important thing is you, your health and your wellbeing. If your mental health is suffering, forget the rest and focus on your own problems. The revolution will wait for you.

" What the spectacle has taken from reality must now be retaken from the spectacle.

I am recovering from a mental problem. I'm not sure what it's is called. It's mentioned somewhere in a David Foster Wallace book. I hear he suffered from something similar.

He had this problem where he would sweat at the slightest mental trigger. And if he worried about sweating it would only make him sweat more. And this might not seem like a big deal to people. We all sweat; it's not so bad right? But it's not like just a little sweat would break out and he'd be just a bit wet, he would start sweating big huge puddles of the stuff.

Imagine if every time you were in a room with someone and they could see your body you would just start to uncontrollably sweat. And if you think about the fact that you are sweating you only sweat more. And then you start worrying about how people are going to perceive you for sweating constantly, creepily, horribly.

It's so horrible it's hard to communicate. You start to worry about it all day, every day. It gets to the point where you base your life around the issue. You avoid any and all situations where the outbreaks of sweat might occur.

Class. Class is a mental strain you can just barely take. Trapped in a room for three hours at a time in close proximity to your classmates. Nowhere to hide, the sweat pouring out of you, the occasional glance from disgusted classmates. Every day.

And forget about getting laid. Not only are you a mental wreck, but suppose somehow you did manage to get laid. What would you do when it came time to cuddle with your partner? Would they ask about the sweat? If they did, what would you say? Would you start bawling to this person you barely know and tell them all about your never-ending nightmare of a life? That'd be a real turn on. No. No. Out of the question.

The question is how to cope. Well one thing that can help is music and books. These can be very therapeutic. They didn't make me happy but they did make me want to live. They made me feel the beauty behind all of my pain. Who could deny the beauty of a Chopin Nocturne or, for that matter, a great Radiohead song?

I listened to this stuff and I realised that despite my depression, despite my being ostracised I still had something quite wonderfully human in me. The sadness expressed in the books I read and the music I listened to helped me regain my humanity.

They left me with the firm belief that I would one day regain some level of self-respect and maybe make it out of this madness alive. After I found out about anarchist-communist politics, I began to realise that the spectacle of modern consumerist society teaches us to hate ourselves for being depressed.

Our society is rife with messages that insist that sadness and loneliness is a problem created because of some sort of individual character flaw instead of a structural one. The spectacle forces everyone to desperately try and meet some standard of human behavior that nobody can actually attain and those that do attain it are often quite miserable.

If you are depressed right now do not feel like it is your own fault. I know that me saying this will not completely make everything better, but start today by thinking about how you are told you are a contemptible worthless nobody, when in fact, you are a human being who deserves to be treated with care and compassion.

You may have fucked up in your life, but who hasn't? This world is merciless and creates insanity in people. You are not to blame. If you think there is a part of you that is morally reprehensible try to fix this but also understand that no matter what you should still treat yourself with respect.

We are bombarded all day long with messages on the television, the internet, movies, everywhere, that tell us to hate ourselves. We must destroy these messages. We must create our own messages of self-respect and pride in our humanity. "What the spectacle has taken from reality must now be retaken from the spectacle. The spectacular expropriators must be expropriated in their turn." Depressed comrades of the world, read, listen, sabotage, and destroy!

Advice from radical mental health professionals

The following section gives tips and advice for navigating the mental health system, receiving the best care for you, and ensuring your voice and your rights are respected by the medical establishment. Although the contributors are based in the UK and the USA, we hope the gist of the advice will apply regardless.

Therapy for Anarchists, Class Warriors, and the Rest of Us
Dr. Charlotte Cooper

In the UK, therapy has roots in middle class philanthropy, and is often accused of being an individualistic response to social problems. This is off-putting to people who feel that the wider social context is relevant to our lives. But therapists are a mixed bunch. Some of us see our work as part of a bigger project of social change. Some of us are working class too, a few are anarchists, and many bring other identities and experience into the mix.

Having a caring space in which you are listened to; understanding what's going on and why you feel so awful, working on meaningful and feasible ways to alleviate that pain are all crucial steps for developing well-being. I am obviously biased because I am a shrink, but I think that counselling and psychotherapy (I use them fairly interchangeably) are primo routes to resolving long-term depression, anxiety, and stress. But getting your hands on some quality, politically engaged psychotherapy when you're too depressed, afraid, or anxious to move is another question.

The Holy Grail
The holy grail: Very cheap or free open-ended counselling/psychotherapy in a style that is compatible with you, with someone local who is clued-in about social marginalisation, and has at least some politics and connection to the communities with whom they work.

Open-ended means that you decide when you're ready to finish. Having someone clued-in means not having to educate the therapist in the basics of your life, and where they will have a grasp of the social context in which you exist, and hopefully some desire for social change. A therapist who has some connection to community will be less likely to patronise or judge. Ideally the therapist should have qualifications, be registered and shouldn't have to work for nothing in horrible conditions (the holy grail is also about recognising their profession, despite popular clichés, as it can be hard way to make a living).

The Reality
If you don't have the money you can approach the therapist of your choice and ask for a reduced price and try to negotiate something affordable. Not all therapists have cheaper

places, there will probably be a wait, and you might find that their version of affordable is still too expensive for you. You might have to try a few people, and the process of negotiating can be quite intimidating.

For free therapy, you can see your doctor to be put on a waiting list for a service about which you have little say, and which is likely to be time-limited (six sessions is common). It's also possible you'll be channelled into an Improving Access to Psychological Therapies programme. While the service can be helpful for some people, you will be using a service which is still in its early days and has come under a lot of fire for its somewhat sausage factory approach to mental health. Plus you might find yourself being seen by someone who's trained in IAPT, but not as a therapist.

You might also find community counselling agencies, but you might be asked to make a financial contribution, and again there are likely to be waiting lists and restrictions on length of service and types of therapies. In community counselling it's common to be seen by trainees rather than experienced therapists.

It can be hard to shop around for someone you like and the service can be a bit hit and miss.

If you are a student or work for a company that has an Employee Assistance Programme that extends to psychotherapy and counselling, you have a better chance of finding free services, but these will probably fall short of the holy grail for many of the reasons outlined above.

The kinds of services I've mentioned here can be really great, but it's worth knowing their limitations, too. Counselling and psychotherapy are somewhat mystified professions, tainted by the stigma of mental illness, which means it's hard to navigate the system and determine what's best for you. All of this can be really exhausting when all you want is to be in a room with someone who will listen, understand, and help you to feel better. Ask around, try not to be intimidated, ask questions and keep going until you find what you're looking for.

Other Routes

The holy grail of therapy may be out of reach, but there are other things you can do to help shift your depression and anxiety. Here are some suggestions that you can mix up and adapt, in no particular order:

Therapy groups exist, but can be quite hard to find, and may be closed to new members. There are many benefits of doing therapy in a group, not least the sense of collective witnessing and information-sharing. They tend to be cheaper than one-to-one sessions. But you also need a really skilled facilitator to help a group function well, and bear in mind that class politics and radical ideas might not be at the top of the agenda, or always welcome. A network of radical therapy groups would be a wonderful thing, but does not currently exist in the UK.

Co-counselling is a grassroots movement in which people pair up and share the roles of counsellor and client, taking turns to speak and listen. It's free. It has roots in a form of counselling that I think is somewhat cultish, but there is no reason that you shouldn't adapt the format to suit yourself. For more information, visit www.co-counselling.org.uk.

Bibliotherapy is a fancy term for reading, specifically reading the kinds of books that might help you feel better. Self-help literature has a bad reputation, often deservedly, but you can still dive in, use the bits that you find useful and discard the rubbish.

You can use other types of literature too, you don't have to limit yourself to one genre; look for poetry, novels, comics, political tracts, etc., that move you or provide some hope or strategies for surviving and thriving. Write about them and keep reading and sharing what you've found, ask people for recommendations. Use the library, read and share things online, lend and borrow.

There are different methods of journaling that can help with depression and anxiety. Some people keep journals to remind themselves of what they have done, you can also use journals to explore particular episodes of your life, or simply to be in the moment and to reflect on your feelings. You can check out 'therapeutic journaling techniques' to find a method you like.

Make stuff, develop public conversations about depression and mental health more generally in the groups and communities you are a part of; try and think about ways in which organisations and activists can be accountable to people's well-being. Get politically active around this stuff, refuse to suffer in isolation and silence, challenge the stigma associated with mental health.

Encourage experimental ways of developing therapy. Alternative means of therapy can be imagined, customised or put into practice. I think that counselling and psychotherapy will remain a remedy for the elite unless we intervene and demand and create services that more readily address our lives and needs and dreams for social transformation.

Finally ... keep going, make it moment-by-moment if you're really struggling. Tell someone. Muster some hope if you can, and use whatever tools are available. The world needs you.

Striving and Thriving: Mental Health on the Radical Left
Tine Phillips

I am a person with lived experience with mental illness, diagnosed bipolar since I was fourteen years old, as well as a mental health professional. It is estimated that one half of all people will develop mental illness in their lifetime. Currently 50 million people (1 in 5) have a diagnosed mental illness in America (not to mention all those who are undiagnosed).

Despite such prevalence, mental illnesses comes with a lot of stigma. As activists we need to fight such stigma. The best way to do that is to talk about it. As a fellow social worker and shame and resiliency researcher, Brené Brown says, "Shame needs three things to grow exponentially in our lives: secrecy, silence, and judgment." As people with mental illness we need to tell people our stories and help normalize it. It takes courage and bravery to put ourselves out there, but it is necessary. We all need to become mental health advocates who combat social stigma if we want this situation to get better.

Politically, a life-long commitment to social justice can be a serious undertaking and means a literal struggle. It comes with many personal as well as political sacrifices that have both psychological and emotional consequences. Of course there are positive mental and emotional benefits of being an activist, but the commitment to the movement comes with both rewards and challenges.

Mental illness is biological, genetic, environmental, and socio-cultural. However, I believe if we lived in a truly socialist society we could see a drastic reduction in mental illness and could even prevent it. Furthermore, we know capitalism creates social alienation and enormous amounts of interpersonal, relational, and social stress on individuals and families.

Not only must we work hard, often at jobs with low pay and long hours, we have many other responsibilities on top of it. We have families, partners and children that we need to help take care of. We have to do chores, feed ourselves and others, and run errands. There is so much to do; we often neglect our own health.

All we can do in the immediate is try to manage the stress, by finding coping skills and decompressing activities. The coping skills can include art, exercise, sleep/naps, socializing with friends and family, eating a slow cooked meal, reading a book, yoga, meditation, relaxation techniques, deep breathing, focusing activities, taking a long walk or hike or going swimming, among other things.

It can be very challenging to overcome the pressures of everyday life, let alone those of being part of an activist movement and community. It is important as an activist that one takes care of oneself and that our community supports us. Burnout is common and all too often we feel our hard work brings too little tangible results. This can lead to disappointment and frustration.

We have to celebrate every victory and recognise people's efforts. Appreciation of others is so important in creating self-esteem and maintaining long-term commitment. We can also stave off burnout by taking breaks from our activism and supporting each other through hard times.

So what is to be done? Our mental health system is far from perfect, too overburdened and too expensive for most people. That is part of why we work as left radicals to change this system into one that works for all people. Unfortunately, in the meantime we have to deal with how things are now.

One thing I advocate is therapy, but it is often cost prohibitive. If one cannot find low cost/sliding scale/income-based therapy, I always recommend workbooks. They teach people step-by-step about the condition which they may have and offer a variety of techniques such as mindfulness to cope with emotional stress and improve overall quality of life. Most therapists would teach these techniques in therapy but you can learn them on your own for a fraction of the cost. And if one technique or workbook doesn't work for you, try another.

Another thing therapists provide is the time and space devoted solely to you and a time to talk/vent and be listened to. You can't find this in a book. But you can find this in other people — friends, family, co-workers, and comrades alike. Find some trusted individuals who are willing to hear you out, provide empathy (not just sympathy), and validation (telling you what you are feeling and thinking is real). Just providing a sounding board of unconditional support can make a world of difference.

I always recommend the rule of threes. Find three reliable people you can go to in a crisis or when something happens that brings you down. Tell your story to those three people, three different times. At the end, you will have released and expressed those feelings and thoughts, will most likely feel better, and hopefully have come up with some solutions.

Of course there is one thing a therapist can provide others can't — and that is education, training, and experience in treating and healing major trauma and psychiatric challenges. There really is no substitute for this. So if you need this, try your best to get it. Oftentimes the expense paid to get this is worth the necessary sacrifices.

Another avenue to increase mental health is using medication. There is much debate about the use of psychotropic medication.

As someone who has bipolar disorder, I know my medication saves my life, both literally and quality-wise. Every individual has to make their own choice whether to try medication and see if it helps. Not everyone has to take medication long term, but some do. I have to take mine the rest of my life, but I am glad there is something out there that profoundly helps me.

Yes, medications are often over-prescribed and developed by big pharmaceutical companies, which are profit-motivated. Yes, doctors can sometimes be pushers because they are getting kick-backs. That is why finding a good doctor to prescribe the right medication is important. This would often be a psychiatrist, who usually does not come cheap. If you can, try to find a lower cost psychiatrist, but if you can't, a general practitioner can prescribe many of the same medications. The caution is they are not trained as well in psychiatric conditions and would not be able to monitor you as well as a psychiatrist could.

Another option that could help and is often more affordable, is herbal remedies and Eastern/alternative medicine. There are many helpful remedies out there worth looking into from vitamins, supplements, teas, essential oils, to acupuncture, acupressure, bio-feedback etc. As well as looking at changes in diet, sleep, and exercise.

Individuals also need social support. If you're in a radical left organisation, develop internal systems to provide this support.

We need to be able to turn to each other in times of need. This prevents burnout and can be a powerful source of intervention in times of crisis. We need to get more involved in people's lives, pay more attention, and be willing to have sometimes uncomfortable conversations with people. We need to focus most on compassion, understanding, and empathy.

Another possible strategy radical left organisations can implement is conflict-management, non-violent communication, and peer counseling. If our organisations used these techniques and taught these skills to all of their members they would be better served by doing so.

Learning how to communicate assertively and not passively, passive-aggressively, or aggressively is very important for any individual or organisation. Our success is wrapped up in our ability to resolve conflicts and reconcile differences. No one gets through this life on their own — we are all interdependent social beings. So let's live our radical values in the here and now and transform ourselves and our organisations to serve each other's needs.

Our organisations can become a model going forward for society and be a source of strength to make us more effective activists. Indeed this can be a protective factor for those with many risk factors for self-harm, homelessness, and suicide. We can be the difference and we are responsible for implementing these suggestions now. •

Dealing with Mental Health Services:
Advice from an anarchist mental health worker

Medical professionals can be hit or miss. If you've talked to your personal doctor about mental health difficulties and feel he/she is being dismissive or isn't taking you seriously, you have the right to ask to be referred to specialist mental health services for an assessment.

The nature of mental health problems are such that it can seem difficult to assert yourself and it can be easy to feel disempowered. This is especially so when dealing with people who might appear to be in positions of authority, like psychiatrists, social workers, or community based mental health workers.

If you feel the need to approach mental health services, have asked your doctor for a referral, or in some other way you come to their attention, the following points might help you to get the most out of it. Remember that service providers are human beings like the rest of us. You are their equal, and your time is as valuable as theirs. You should expect to be treated as an equal, with respect and dignity.

Try and be as clear as possible when talking about your problems. You should get the most help and the most benefit if those you are asking for help under stand what's wrong and what sort of help you feel you need. If there are specific things that have helped you in the past (a certain medication, talking therapies, group work etc.), make this known, and try and think about other things that you feel would help.

Also make sure things are explained clearly to you, in a way you understand. If a course of medication is suggested, ask questions about it, and try and make sure that potential negative side effects are explained as well as hoped-for positive effects. If you are given a diagnosis, try and ensure that the symptoms, characteristics, prognosis and implications are clearly explained.

If you feel that social circumstances (poverty, threat of eviction, isolation, substance use issues, etc.) are contributing to your mental ill-health, make this known. Services have a duty to support you with these problems if your mental health is such that you can't do it yourself. Being given anti-depressants and sent back to the root problems that caused the depression, for example, is not good enough.

Remember that you have the right to complain. If you disagree with any decision, diagnosis, course of action or treatment plan or you feel you're not being listened to or taken seriously, talk to the people involved and let them know, if you feel confident doing so.

A trusted friend or family member, or an advocacy worker can help you here, too. If you're still unhappy, you can make a formal complaint, you can ask for a second opinion, or you can request a change of doctor.

Health boards have a duty to publish complaints procedures, and copies should be available at local community mental health team resource centres, and normally online as well.

You should be at the centre of any decision making. Do your best to make sure that your views are taken into account. Taking someone else (again, a friend or family member, or an advocacy worker) who understands your situation along to appointments can help with this.

Remember that nothing can be imposed on you against your will unless you are subject to mental health legislation, and certain steps have been taken allowing decisions to be made by professionals. Even in this situation, you do still have certain legal rights, which should be clearly explained, and you should still be at the centre of decision making as much as this is possible.

If you find yourself subject to mental health legislation (detained in hospital, given medical treatment against your will etc.), make sure, as best you can, that the process is explained clearly in a way that you understand, including what your rights are.

Service providers and those responsible for the compulsory measures have a legal duty to explain this to you. Again, having someone else who is on your side (a friend, family member or advocacy worker) can help. If you are unhappy, you are entitled to free legal advice and representation, and in most cases have the right to appeal.

Remember that mental health service providers are there to help you.

Anything they do should benefit you, and should be intended to get the best outcome possible for you. If you are unhappy at any point, you can seek advice and support from friends, family, other service users and independent advocacy and mental health organisations.

Essays on Organisational Culture and Mental Health

Be Good to Your Comrades: Why Being a Prick is Counterrevolutionary

Is it just me or do anarchists have a tendency to be a bunch of pricks? Actually, I know it's not just me. Because I've had this conversation, in whispered tones, with a few other anarchists. And they agree.

Let me back up. Anarchists can also be some of the nicest people I know. Many pour their time and energy, sweat and tears, into building revolution— driven by the deep desire to make the world a better place. On the whole they are caring, altruistic, generous, and giving.

But my goodness, can they also be harsh, condescending, and sometimes downright bullies. This hurtful behavior mostly arises in political disagreements. Which means it arises quite regularly. Because anarchists get into a lot of political disagreements. Not least of all with each other.

I have a feeling, dear comrade, that you will be all too familiar with what I'm talking about. You see it in your own organisation. You see it on the internet forums. Maybe you've seen it in yourself. Why is this type of behavior so common? Is it because anarchists are used to having our ideas attacked so it's put us in the habit of lashing out defensively?

Is it because many anarchists are thick skinned (a helpful asset when you base much of your life on an unpopular view) and so we don't realise that words and tones which wouldn't phase us will hurt our thinner skinned comrades? Is it because we're so full of bitterness about the current state of the world that we take it out on others?

For some of us, maybe it's that we have such distaste for hippies that we strive to be as unlike them as we can, including by disregarding all concern with (gag) "feelings"? Whatever the reason, it's got to stop.

It hurts people. It can wound and even scar people. I know two anarchists who are seriously depressed in large part due to the pattern of interpersonal brutality in their organisation.

One frequently considers quitting because of it. I know of two others who refuse to join the organisation because of bullying they either experienced or witnessed. And so it is that interpersonal meanness by anarchists can, should, and must be recognised for what it is: counterrevolutionary. Why? Because it sabotages our efforts to create revolution.

When anarchists act like pricks they drive others away from revolutionary organising. Nobody likes being around people who make them feel like crap.

For those not driven away, this subtle bullying can beat us into a pit of depression and injured self-confidence, and it's damn hard to meet the responsibilities of revolutionary activity when you're depressed, or share your ideas in meetings or volunteer for challenging tasks if your self-confidence is in the toilet. Meanness causes our numbers to be fewer and our comrades to be less effective.

Successful revolution requires that the vast majority of the working class embrace anarchism. This won't happen if the extremely tiny minority who currently have anarchist politics push everyone else away because we don't know how to have a political disagreement without resorting to humiliation or intimidation, or because we ridicule and ostracise those with political views we (rightly or wrongly) look down on.

This doesn't mean we should not express criticism or disagreements. This is the only way to change minds. But always be friendly and respectful even— no, especially— during debate.

One way to deal with this problem is the anarchist principle of collective responsibility. If members of an organisation see that someone is beginning to speak or act in a disrespectful way, it should be an obligation to intervene by pointing this out. This need not have any purpose except to bring it to everyone's attention. But formal consequences can be used if desired.

Perhaps the second time someone is called-out they should be required to stop speaking and be bumped down a spot on the speaker's list (giving them a chance to calm down and reflect before finishing whatever point they were making).

A third warning could require being bumped down two spots, and so on—although at some point, if it isn't letting up, perhaps they should be asked to leave the meeting. If consequences are used, there might be a risk that calling-out the disrespectfulness of others be used dishonestly just to interrupt what someone was saying.

In that case, a rule can be made that at least one other person must agree that disrespect is present. It helps if someone is assigned the prime responsibility of being watchful of the respect level during a meeting. (This person should be someone other than the chair, because chairs have other things they need to pay attention to.) But anyone in the meeting should call-out disrespect as soon as they see it. And, like any role of importance, the role of respect-watcher should be rotated.

Things become more difficult outside of meetings during informal hang-outs, especially if they involve alcohol. With the respect-watcher off duty, the collective responsibility of the group to make sure interactions are friendly and respectful must be at the forefront of everyone's mind.

If someone has a pattern of intimidating or humiliating others and it doesn't show signs of going away even after ongoing intervention, this person should be expelled from the organisation or at least suspended. Whatever assets they bring to the organisation, it does more harm than good to keep a bully around.

This collection of articles is meant, in part, to help guide us in how we, as anarchists, can support our comrades who might be depressed or otherwise dealing with mental health issues. I believe the number one thing we can do is simply be good to each other. Let's stop giving our comrades yet another reason to be depressed.

A Proposal for Collective Accommodation

I am one of many class struggle anarchists with mental illness. I am a member of an anarchist political organisation and have been for the past five years. In recent months, we have begun discussing developing a 'code of conduct' around member behaviour.

Because my particular mental illness involves some pretty disruptive and inappropriate behaviour at times, I would like to explore some ideas on how organisations can accommodate people like me, while also maintaining the functioning of the organisation. In my experience, this is generally not done well.

So, for this piece, I would first like to lay out some of the pitfalls I have noticed organisations have come up against in addressing this. I would then like to make a proposal for 'collective accommodation' and explain why it might offer a better structure for support.

First of all, I would like to be very clear that I in no way wish to reinforce any stereotypes around people with a mental illness being disruptive or having behaviour that is problematic to others. For many, many people, this is not the case. For me, however, I am diagnosed with borderline personality disorder.

Briefly, BPD involves very extreme emotions, which tend to last very short periods of time. Due to painful and intense emotions, and often a tendency toward impulsiveness, many people with BPD struggle with issues such as self-injury, suicide ideation, drug/ alcohol abuse, etc.

For me, many of the issues and conflicts that come with being in an organisation can be very difficult, and at times I have used these types of negative behaviours as ways of coping, with detrimental effects on others.

So again, I would like to be clear that the ideas I'm proposing are in no way relevant to everyone who deals with mental health issues—but are to me, and potentially to other situations in various activist groups. In my experience, anarchist/activist groups generally do a pretty poor job of dealing with disruptive behaviour, particularly when some aspect of mental health is involved.

Generally, the trajectory I have seen is that groups tend to start out without any formal standards around behaviour, but more of an implied norm that everyone is expected to follow. When issues do emerge, groups tend to go one of two ways. One is to create some sort of 'code of conduct' setting out expectations around behaviour. Often, these conversations are presented as general, but are really in reference to a few members who are seen to demonstrate some sort of behavioural issue disruptive to the group.

When a mental health issue is raised, little real support or understanding seems to be available. Another way is to "accommodate" members who have disruptive behaviour by allowing them to remain in the group. Often, this accommodation looks like tolerating someone without truly including them (politically and/or in the social life of the group) or listening to their ideas.

At times, it takes a very negative direction, when individuals who act in aggressive, demeaning ways toward others are allowed to continue to so, simply because these behaviours are attributed to a mental health issue. In the worst cases, I have seen individuals attempt to excuse oppressive (sexist, racist, etc) behaviour as a mental health issue, and get a pass—while alienating and oppressing others in the group.

In my view, both these approaches are flawed. Rather than addressing the complex balance of group and individual needs, they take an all or nothing approach—either the entire responsibility is on the individual to meet the standard or it is on the group to accommodate. They ignore the complexity of interactions—that the group itself may be a stressor, or that individuals may have other complex things going on in their lives. While different, both these approaches tend to have the same result of failing to offer real support and accountability.

I propose that, as anarchists, we can do better. Although it can be difficult at times, I think that 'letting the politics lead' with regards to what initially appear like personal topics—such as mental health—can be useful. In this case, I would draw on mutual aid and collective responsibility to propose a form of 'collective accommodation'.

The model I propose would balance personal and collective responsibility to support members who struggle with selfregulation to meet standards that are realistic for them. It would also take into account that the organisation itself and other members may act as stressors, and that a person's behaviour is not all on them. Finally, I believe it offers an ultimately positive view of people who struggle with mental illness, as it is both compassionate to their struggles and respectful of their strengths.

So, rather than a code of conduct approach—or perhaps, written in with it— the group would also allow individuals to take leadership in defining and getting support for their own participation.

This would allow members to set realistic goals that don't expect perfect behaviour and accept and work with complex factors such as mental health. Some examples of issues that could be included might be:

1. Understanding: How does the individual understand their own behaviour and situation? What is important for other members to know? I think explaining what is behind certain behaviours might help other members be more sensitive to potential triggers, as well as understand generally what is at play.
2. Meeting strategies: Meetings can often be difficult. What are our expectations around conduct in meetings? What can the group put in place to better accommodate members who might be more easily overwhelmed? For example, changing meeting structures to allow for breaks during stressful topics. It is important here to talk about responsibility—is the individual responsible for deciding what they can or can't deal with? What role do other group members have?
3. Expectations around conflict: Conflict can be very triggering for many people. What can be put in place to make sure we are addressing the real political/strategic issues, without creating an unhealthy or unsafe situation for members? What responsibilities do different members take on in ensuring conflict is handled in productive ways?

4. Expectations around political work: Sometimes those with real barriers to participation, such as mental health concerns, are perceived as 'flaking out' when they don't complete tasks. At the same time, having to pick up extra responsibilities or dealing with the repercussions of important work not getting done can be stressful for other members. How do we manage this? What channels are available if we need to shift things around? How do we make sure everyone isn't stretched to their limit, so there is someone extra to take things on if it is too much?

There may be many others, depending on the particular individuals and situations involved. Generally, however, the principles would be to be realistic and not expect perfection; to try to understand and accommodate individuals; and to talk about sharing responsibility—accommodation doesn't mean making excuses, and having a mental illness doesn't mean that people are incapable.

It may just mean we need support to participate. Implementing this model would also mean having difficult discussions around our limitations—potentially suggesting people seek professional support if needed, as well as looking at what behaviours—such as those that are overtly oppressive to others—we really can't tolerate, regardless of factors involved, and would require us to ask people to leave.

In most cases, however, the goal would be to offer support so that members not only remain in political organisations, but thrive in them. Despite some unique challenges that come as an anarchists who deal with mental illness, we also bring a whole lot of resilience, insight, sensitivity, dedication, and bravery from our life experiences to our groups and our political work.

And all anarchists have a lot we can learn from creatively supporting and accommodating each other, lessons that will hopefully carry over into broader struggles.

Tips and discussion topics for groups and organisations

Dealing with mental health issues should be a matter of basic solidarity. It's something we can do to help each other and it's good for us a movement, too: combating burnout and creating a healthy culture of discussion, openness, and support.

The following list is far from exhaustive and is, in fact, more a series of suggestions that groups might consider in formulating a policy and practice of addressing mental health issues and supporting members dealing with depression, anxiety, and overall emotional stress.

While there are probably no definitive answers for how to build such a culture, having discussions and creating structures are necessary first steps. With that in mind, here's a list of potential discussion points which relate to political activity, organisation, and mental health:

1. Are our groups open about mental health issues? Do members feel comfortable discussing their emotional health or taking a short mental health break? If not, why not? Do we casually use words that are derived expressions which denigrate the mentally ill?

Do we have networks/structures in place to support those who need it? Would a sort of buddy system be beneficial? Should there be a named person or people whose role it is to ensure mental health issues are addressed by the wider organisation?

Of course in all of this, there's a fine line to be walked. The reality is that there's a stigma associated with mental illness. This means that not everyone will feel comfortable talking about such things, even in what's hopefully a sympathetic situation. That's to be expected, but it shouldn't be an excuse for us not creating a culture of openness and support when it comes to issues of mental (as well as physical) health.

2. Are our meeting places and social activities conducive to those who may be dealing with emotional stress?

Far too often, the bar/pub is the default place for our meetings. This is not going to helpful to those who've suffered from addiction in the past or who may want to avoid crowds for whatever reason. If we're going to be an open movement, it's imperative we have open, accountable meeting spaces. Organisationally, are we cliquish? Do we use a lot of alienating jargon?

Are new members consciously integrated into the internal life of the organisation? As a movement what can we do to alleviate the stress of our members who have more on their plate than just politics? Is childcare available at meetings? Do meeting spaces have disability access? Are our meetings short, concise, and structured or do they drag on interminably?

Similarly, do all our social functions revolve around alcohol or a particular musical subculture? A variety of social activities will attract a variety of participants.

Regardless of whether someone is suffering from depression or not, it's going to be really helpful if there's a choice of social activities on offer. It will help people open up and feel like they're part of the larger group, creating the bonds that allow us to tackle issues like mental health.

3. Do we proactively undertake activities which are good for the mental health of everyone? This can be simple things like incorporating physical activity into the social life of organisations.

We can have regular sporting events or offer self-defense classes. Or we can encourage members to use their creativity to benefit the movement. Everything from poetry and art to music and theatre can be therapeutic and there's no reason such activities can't be a part of what we do. They are not only good for those of us suffering mental illness, but for all of us, not least because they remind us of the good, shared human things for which we are all fighting.

Credits

About Our Contributors

Most of the editors and writers participating in this project have chosen to remain anonymous, but please visit and support the websites of the many other writers and artists/illustrators who've volunteered their work:

LYN X (aka Espa Idlenomore Love), designer/production editor of the US version of this book, is a founding director of Edmonton Small Press Association (ESPA), a long-disgruntled member of the arts-precariat (who insisted we include artist/writer credits to anyone that wants them), an intersectional activist, and a resourceful single mom who firmly believes the arts to be vital tools for positive social change.

BAGGELBOY (aka Alan Rogerson) is the excellent cover artist. Check out more of his great work at baggelboy.com or facebook.com/thebaggelboy.

STEPHANIE MCMILLAN (page 7) is an award-wining U.S. illustrator, well known in the environmental & social justice movement for her Minimum Security & Code Green comics. See more of her work and order her many books, including the brand-new Capitalism Must Die! at stephaniemcmillan.org

DR. CHARLOTTE COOPER (page 24) is a psychotherapist/counsellor based in East London. See her website at charlottecooper.net

TINA PHILLIPS (page 26) is a social worker with a master's degree in the field.

EDMONTON SMALL PRESS ASSOCIATION (ESPA) is a registered, non-profit independent media and activist-arts society with a socially-conscious mandate, and has been an active participant in Edmonton's community arts, social justice & environmental communities since 1998.

ESPA maintains a growing Small Press Library and Archive; operates a local Infoshop/Distro; presents thought-provoking and award-winning art exhibits, film screenings & special guest speakers; and also undertakes other special projects, such as community Murals and small publishing projects as time permits.

ESPA is 100% volunteer-operated and does not receive any government or corporate operational funding. The group gratefully accepts small press and activist-art donations from around the world, including zines, political graphics & poster art, mail art, art/documentary DVDs, and more.

The Editors of Class Struggle and Mental Health: Live to Fight Another Day would like to thank **LIBCOM.ORG** for their instrumental role in bringing this pamphlet together. libcom.org is a huge online resource comprising a library, forums, and blogs. It exists both to promote the ideas of libertarian communism and to give pissed-off workers a space to come together and support each other in the fight for a better world.

Readers can also find & join Libcom on facebook at facebook.com/libcom.org.

FREEDOM PRESS was founded by a group of friends including Charlotte Wilson and Peter Kropotkin, who were already publishing Freedom newspaper. It has operated, with short breaks, ever since and has been at its home in Tower Hamlets for the last 70 years.

An independent, radical co-op controlled by its volunteers and part-time staff, Freedom runs Britain's oldest anarchist press and its largest bookshop.

Alongside our own extensive back catalogue of classic works we stock thousands of books, newspapers and pamphlets on everything from history to sex, philosophy to workers' struggles, fiction to anti-fascism, as well as the latest magazines, periodicals and newsletters from all the major anarchist and radical groups.

ALSO BY...

Freedom Press

Anarchism without
the syndicalism

£5

Anarchism in
the everyday

£7.50

Red Action on
the '80s street war

£15

Loveable cartoon
meets class struggle

£8

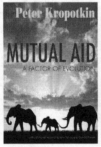

Famed rebuttal of
social Darwinism

£15

Biography of the
iconic 1910s rebel

£9.50

History of the British
anarchist movement

£15

A concise tale of
anarcho-syndicalism

£5

The surprising politics
of Herbert Read

£6

DIRECT SALES AND ENQUIRIES

Freedom Press
Angel Alley,
84b Whitechapel High
Street, London
E1 7QX

Telephone
(020) 7247-9249
or (07952 157-742)

Email
admin@
freedompress.org.uk

Web
freedompress.org.uk

Social media
@freedom_paper
facebook.com/
freedombookshop

Trade orders may
be placed via Central
Books:

Central Books Ltd,
99 Wallis Road, London
E9 5LN

Tel 44 (0)20 8525 8800
Fax 44 (0)20 8525 8879
contactus@centralbooks.
com

www.centralbooks.com